Exploring American History ①

Reading, Vocabulary, and Test-taking Skills

Teacher's Manual

Student Book Authors

Phil LeFaivre

and

Flo Decker

Teacher's Manual Writer

Stephen Handorf

Exploring American History: Reading, Vocabulary, and Test-taking Skill TM 1

Published by McGraw-Hill ESL/ELT, a business unit of the McGraw-Hill Companies, Inc., 1221 Avenue of the Americas, New York, NY 10020. Copyright © 2004 by The McGraw-Hill Companies, Inc. All rights reserved. No part of this publication may be reproduced or distributed in any form or by any means, or stored in a database or retrieval system, without the prior written consent of The McGraw-Hill Companies, Inc., including, but not limited to, in any network or other electronic storage or transmission, or broadcast for distance learning.

ISBN: 0-07-285468-5

Editorial director: Tina B. Carver
Senior managing editor: Erik Gundersen
Sr. developmental editor: Stephen Handorf
Developmental editor: Linda O'Roke
Editorial assistant: David Averbach
Production manager: Juanita Thompson
Cover design: Four Lakes Colorgraphics Inc.
Interior design: Acento Visual
Art: Wilkinson Studios

Table of Contents

Introduction

The Teacher's Manual to *Exploring American History 1: Reading, Vocabulary, and Test-taking Skills* includes chapter quizzes for each chapter. It also includes a complete answer key to the exercises found in *Exploring American History 1.*

Chapter Quizzes

- There are 16 quizzes, one for each chapter of *Exploring American History 1.* The quizzes are easy to give and easy to correct.
- The quizzes are designed as a review of the general concepts covered in the book. Each quiz is worth ten points.
  - Part A consists of six vocabulary questions worth one point each. Students are asked to complete sentences with missing words from a list of six of the ten vocabulary items presented in each chapter.
  - Part B consists of four reading comprehension questions worth one point each. One question focuses on the main idea of the reading, two focus on important details, and one requires students to make inferences based on what they have read. The quizzes do not require students to memorize specific dates or obscure names.
- Each quiz takes approximately 15 minutes to complete.
- There is a complete answer key for each quiz.

Answer Key for *Exploring American History 1*

- There is a complete answer key to the student book.
- Answers are given, when possible, for the Get Ready to Read, Check Your Comprehension, Build Your Vocabulary, Improve Your Reading Skills, and Expand Your Vocabulary sections.

Answer Key for *Exploring American History 1* Workshops

- There is a complete answer key to the eight workshops that appear throughout the student book.

Name_____ Date_____ Score_____

A. VOCABULARY CHECK

Choose a word from the box to complete each sentence.

drought	hurricane	inhabitants	preserve	remote	settle

1. The flood got worse. So the town's _____ moved up the mountain.

2. It takes three days to reach the _____ island by boat.

3. The _____ broke windows in houses near the ocean.

4. The national park tries to _____ the forest's natural beauty.

5. Many people who come to live in the U.S. decide to _____ in California.

6. The plants dried up and died during the long _____.

B. COMPREHENSION CHECK

Think about "The Mystery of the Ancient Pueblo People." Fill in the correct bubble.

7. The Ancient Pueblo people built their cities _____.

   Ⓐ under the ground   Ⓒ in the side of cliffs

   Ⓑ on the top of hills   Ⓓ near a lake

8. Where did the Ancient Pueblo people get their baskets?

   Ⓐ They bought them.   Ⓒ They stole them.

   Ⓑ They found them.   Ⓓ They made them.

9. Why do scientists think the Ancient Pueblo people left their cities?

   Ⓐ It was too hot there.   Ⓒ They got sick and died.

   Ⓑ Enemies made them leave.   Ⓓ There was not enough rain or food.

10. Which sentence about the Ancient Pueblo people is probably true?

   Ⓐ They had some enemies.   Ⓒ They did not have many skills.

   Ⓑ Farming was very easy for them.   Ⓓ They were afraid of water.

Name_____ Date_____ Score_____

A. VOCABULARY CHECK

Choose a word from the box to complete each sentence.

| canal | cruel | ordered | peninsula | permanent | rumor |

1. Florida is a(n) _____ with water on three sides of it.

2. The _____ man made his animals work hard without water.

3. I heard a(n) _____ that Carol is leaving, but she hasn't told me yet.

4. Write your name with _____ ink so that it will not wash off.

5. The general _____ his soldiers to stay and fight.

6. They built a(n) _____ through Panama for ships to go from the Atlantic Ocean to the Pacific Ocean.

B. COMPREHENSION CHECK

Think about "Ponce de León and the Fountain of Youth." Fill in the correct bubble.

7. Ponce de León looked for _____ for many years until he died.

    Ⓐ the Gulf Stream   Ⓒ slaves

    Ⓑ food   Ⓓ a magic fountain

8. Ponce de León was from _____.

    Ⓐ South America   Ⓒ Puerto Rico

    Ⓑ Spain   Ⓓ Florida

9. Ponce de León found _____ near the coast of Florida.

    Ⓐ a big road   Ⓒ a powerful ocean current

    Ⓑ the fountain of youth   Ⓓ gold coins

10. Why did Ponce de León die?

    Ⓐ He was a bad leader.   Ⓒ Native people did not like him.

    Ⓑ He liked gold more than food.   Ⓓ He got old and sick.

Name _____ Date _____ Score _____

A. VOCABULARY CHECK

Choose a word from the box to complete each sentence.

colonies	customers	employer	jealous	profit	purchased

1. They _____ their house in May and moved in June.

2. Veronica was _____ of her cousin because he had a new bike.

3. The company was very successful last year and made a big _____.

4. Business was not good today. Only three _____ came into the store.

5. England started _____ all over the world and sent people to live in them.

6. It is sometimes difficult to go to work for a new _____.

B. COMPREHENSION CHECK

Think about "New York City, the Money Machine." Fill in the correct bubble.

7. New Amsterdam was _____.

   Ⓐ a poor colony   Ⓒ a successful colony

   Ⓑ an Indian settlement   Ⓓ an English colony

8. The first Dutch people came to America to _____.

   Ⓐ make money   Ⓒ have more space

   Ⓑ have religious freedom   Ⓓ escape a cruel government

9. New York got its name from _____.

   Ⓐ a Native American word   Ⓒ the name of a trading company

   Ⓑ the name of a Dutch city   Ⓓ the English King's brother

10. The people in the early colony of New York _____.

   Ⓐ didn't think the old wall was important   Ⓒ sold stocks on Wall Street

   Ⓑ spoke only Dutch   Ⓓ didn't want to work hard

Name_____ Date_____ Score_____

A. VOCABULARY CHECK

Choose a word from the box to complete each sentence.

approval	hostile	seized	tension	treaty	wounded

1. Six people were _____ in the fight and went to the hospital.

2. Both groups want the same land, so there is a lot of _____ between them.

3. Leaders from both sides signed the _____ to end the war.

4. You have to get _____ from the principal to put up a poster.

5. Police came into the house and _____ the illegal drugs and guns.

6. The people in the town were _____ and made me feel afraid.

B. COMPREHENSION CHECK

Think about "The Battles of Lexington and Concord." Fill in the correct bubble.

7. Why was the battle at Lexington so important?
   - Ⓐ Ten people were killed there.
   - Ⓑ The English beat the colonists.
   - Ⓒ It started the American Revolution.
   - Ⓓ Paul Revere was there.

8. Paul Revere rode to Lexington to _____.
   - Ⓐ watch the fight
   - Ⓑ help the English soldiers
   - Ⓒ tell the colonists to get ready
   - Ⓓ escape from Boston

9. At Lexington there were _____.
   - Ⓐ more English soldiers than colonists
   - Ⓑ more colonists than English soldiers
   - Ⓒ only colonists
   - Ⓓ very few people on either side

10. Why did the King say that colonists needed approval for their town meetings?
    - Ⓐ He was afraid of colonists.
    - Ⓑ He wanted to come.
    - Ⓒ He thought that meetings were silly.
    - Ⓓ He wanted his governor to be busy.

Name_____ Date_____ Score_____

A. VOCABULARY CHECK

Choose a word from the box to complete each sentence.

candidate	citizen	debate	defeated	document	representatives

1. If you are not a _____, you cannot vote in national elections.

2. Read this _____. It has a lot of important information in it.

3. I did not want to vote for either _____, but I had to choose one.

4. In the U.S., we elect _____ to go to Washington, D.C. and make our laws.

5. The two groups had a long _____ about whether to build a new school.

6. Our football team _____ the team from the other school. The score was 42 to 12.

B. COMPREHENSION CHECK

Think about "The Declaration of Independence." Fill in the correct bubble.

7. The Declaration of Independence says _____, not kings, should make laws.
   - Ⓐ presidents
   - Ⓑ Thomas Jefferson
   - Ⓒ the people
   - Ⓓ George Washington

8. There were _____ American colonies in 1776.
   - Ⓐ 30
   - Ⓑ 13
   - Ⓒ 15
   - Ⓓ 12

9. The Declaration of Independence was signed _____.
   - Ⓐ before the colonies were independent
   - Ⓑ after the American Revolution
   - Ⓒ in Boston, Massachusetts
   - Ⓓ by the King of England

10. Which sentence about Thomas Jefferson is probably true?
    - Ⓐ He did not have very much money.
    - Ⓑ He liked the King of England.
    - Ⓒ He did not like to write.
    - Ⓓ Other colonists liked him.

Name_____ Date_____ Score_____

A. VOCABULARY CHECK

Choose a word from the box to complete each sentence.

capital	career	Congress	identical	instruments	Supreme Court

1. The dentist uses special _____ to clean my teeth.

2. _____ makes all the national laws for the United States.

3. These two shirts are _____. I don't know which one is yours.

4. The country's most important government buildings are in the _____.

5. The _____ must decide if the other court's decision was right.

6. Antonio's mother had a long _____ as a teacher.

B. COMPREHENSION CHECK

Think about "Benjamin Banneker: Self-Taught Genius." Fill in the correct bubble.

7. Benjamin Banneker is famous today because _____.

    Ⓐ he made a clock

    Ⓑ he helped plan an important city

    Ⓒ he collected stamps

    Ⓓ he was good at math

8. How did Banneker learn to make a clock?

    Ⓐ He took another clock apart.

    Ⓑ He read a book about clocks.

    Ⓒ He watched someone make a clock.

    Ⓓ A friend explained it to him.

9. Why did Banneker have to draw the plans for Washington, D.C., again?

    Ⓐ The first plans had too many parts.

    Ⓑ The first designer died before he finished the plans.

    Ⓒ The first plans burned up in a fire.

    Ⓓ The designer took the first plans away.

10. When Benjamin Banneker was alive, most African Americans _____.

    Ⓐ could read and write

    Ⓑ did not go to school

    Ⓒ studied the stars

    Ⓓ made clocks

Name_____ Date_____ Score_____

A. VOCABULARY CHECK

Choose a word from the box to complete each sentence.

captured	courageous	desert	journey	nutritious	valley

1. The farm was at the bottom of a _____ with green hills all around.

2. Police _____ the killers after only three days.

3. You have to be very _____ to go to new and dangerous places.

4. In the _____ it is hot during the day, but it gets cold at night.

5. You should eat _____ food to stay healthy.

6. Lewis and Clark went on a _____ from St. Louis to the Pacific Ocean.

B. COMPREHENSION CHECK

Think about "Sacagawea and the Path to the Sea." Fill in the correct bubble.

7. Why was Sacagawea so important to Lewis and Clark?
   - Ⓐ She was very beautiful.
   - Ⓑ She could speak to other Native Americans for them.
   - Ⓒ She was a good fighter.
   - Ⓓ She knew how to read and write English.

8. President _____ asked Lewis and Clark to take the trip.
   - Ⓐ George Washington
   - Ⓑ John Adams
   - Ⓒ Thomas Jefferson
   - Ⓓ Abraham Lincoln

9. _____ gave Lewis and Clark the things they needed to cross the mountains.
   - Ⓐ Sacagawea
   - Ⓑ Sacagawea's mother
   - Ⓒ Sacagawea's husband
   - Ⓓ Sacagawea's brother

10. In 1804 _____ in the places that Lewis and Clark visited.
   - Ⓐ there were no roads
   - Ⓑ there were a few large highways
   - Ⓒ the roads were not very good
   - Ⓓ there were many good roads

Name_____ Date_____ Score_____

A. VOCABULARY CHECK

Choose a word from the box to complete each sentence.

amateur	biography	fiction	patriotic	released	surrender

1. Jessica is just a(n) _____ singer, but she is getting better.

2. The army kept fighting and did not _____.

3. On July Fourth, people carry flags and sing _____ songs.

4. I'm reading about Francis Scott Key's life in his _____.

5. I like to read _____ because anything can happen.

6. We kept the sick bird in a cage until it was better. Then we _____ it.

B. COMPREHENSION CHECK

Think about "The Star-Spangled Banner: Our National Anthem." Fill in the correct bubble.

7. Why did Francis Scott Key write *The Star-Spangled Banner?*

    Ⓐ He was angry with the English soldiers.   Ⓒ He was proud of America.

    Ⓑ He wanted a song to play at baseball games.   Ⓓ He wanted to become famous.

8. Why was Key in Baltimore Harbor during the fight?

    Ⓐ He was helping his friend.   Ⓒ He wanted to watch the fighting.

    Ⓑ He was leaving Baltimore.   Ⓓ He was just coming to Baltimore.

9. Key was _____ when he started to write *The Star-Spangled Banner.*

    Ⓐ in the city of Baltimore   Ⓒ on a ship

    Ⓑ in Washington, D.C.   Ⓓ in Fort McHenry

10. Why did Eben Appleton probably give the Fort McHenry flag away?

    Ⓐ He didn't want it anymore.   Ⓒ He needed money.

    Ⓑ He wanted to share it.   Ⓓ He didn't know it was important.

Name_____ Date_____ Score_____

A. VOCABULARY CHECK

Choose a word from the box to complete each sentence.

authority	democracy	dictatorship	loyalty	revenge	survivors

1. In a(n) _____ we elect our political leaders.

2. The police have the _____ to close the road if they need to.

3. The plane crashed and there were no _____.

4. Jane did not leave her husband when he went to jail. That showed a lot of

_____.

5. The young man wanted _____ against the people who killed his father.

6. Life under the cruel _____ was hard.

B. COMPREHENSION CHECK

Think about "Remembering the Alamo." Fill in the correct bubble.

7. The men who fought at the Alamo _____.

   Ⓐ stopped the Mexican army   Ⓒ fought the Mexican army again later

   Ⓑ were all killed   Ⓓ made the first Texas flag

8. In 1830 in the Mexican territory of Tejas, _____.

   Ⓐ almost everyone was Spanish   Ⓒ almost no one spoke Spanish

   Ⓑ there were more Mexicans than Americans   Ⓓ there were more Americans than Mexicans

9. Antonio López de Santa Anna _____.

   Ⓐ was the ruler of Mexico   Ⓒ died near the San Jacinto River

   Ⓑ was the governor of Texas   Ⓓ was killed at the Alamo

10. Most American settlers in Texas _____ about what happened at the Alamo.

   Ⓐ did not know   Ⓒ were angry

   Ⓑ did not care   Ⓓ were happy

Name_____ Date_____ Score_____

A. VOCABULARY CHECK

Choose a word from the box to complete each sentence.

accused	legend	majority	opposed	refused	trial

1. Many people _____ the idea, but it will be a law anyway.

2. There will be a(n) _____ to decide whether the men are guilty.

3. According to a(n) _____, a cow started a fire that burned down the city of Chicago.

4. Tony _____ me of taking his book, but I didn't do it.

5. Natalie _____ to tell me where she was going.

6. A(n) _____ of voters want to build the new road, so it will be built next year.

B. COMPREHENSION CHECK

Think about "The Trail of Tears." Fill in the correct bubble.

7. The journey on the Trail of Tears was _____.

    Ⓐ short and easy   Ⓒ long, but easy

    Ⓑ short, but difficult   Ⓓ long and difficult

8. At first, _____ of the Cherokee people refused to move.

    Ⓐ all   Ⓒ a few

    Ⓑ most   Ⓓ none

9. During the trip to Indian Territory, the weather was very _____.

    Ⓐ cold   Ⓒ dry

    Ⓑ hot   Ⓓ nice

10. Why did the Native Americans have to give up their land and move?

    Ⓐ The government wanted them to build new cities in the west.   Ⓒ The places where they were living were dangerous.

    Ⓑ The land in the west was better.   Ⓓ The government wanted their land.

Name_____ Date_____ Score_____

A. VOCABULARY CHECK

Choose a word from the box to complete each sentence.

eventually	infection	legislature	precise	radical	therapy

1. Over half of the members of the state _____ voted for the law.

2. I got a(n) _____ on my big toe, and it got red and swollen.

3. After the accident, Ken needed _____ to learn to walk again.

4. The teacher's instructions were very _____, so we knew exactly what to do.

5. The story might be confusing at first, but _____ you'll understand it.

6. If we make too many _____ changes, people will be upset. We need to make changes more slowly.

B. COMPREHENSION CHECK

Think about "Dorothea Dix: Defender of Mentally Ill People." Fill in the correct bubble.

7. Dorothea Dix thought that mentally ill people _____.

   Ⓐ could be cured

   Ⓑ should be in jail

   Ⓒ did not feel heat or cold

   Ⓓ should be punished

8. Dix visited _____ in Massachusetts.

   Ⓐ one jail

   Ⓑ many jails

   Ⓒ only a few jails

   Ⓓ no jails

9. Dix wanted to _____.

   Ⓐ have her own hospital

   Ⓑ get rid of hospitals for mentally ill people

   Ⓒ become famous

   Ⓓ open more hospitals for mentally ill people

10. In the early 1800s, most people thought that mentally ill people _____.

   Ⓐ were equal to other people

   Ⓑ should be treated very kindly

   Ⓒ did not need to be treated well

   Ⓓ could be cured

Name_____ Date_____ Score_____

A. VOCABULARY CHECK

Choose a word from the box to complete each sentence.

continent	departs	doubted	Hemisphere	influence	population

1. Li has visited every _____ except Australia and Antarctica.

2. Cleo said that her mother was a princess, but most people _____ her story.

3. North and South America are both in the Western _____.

4. Most parents have a lot of _____ on how their children behave.

5. The _____ of India is over one billion people.

6. Our train _____ at 7:15 and arrives in New York at 8:30.

B. COMPREHENSION CHECK

Think about "Gold Fever Hits California." Fill in the correct bubble.

7. During the gold rush, _____.

   Ⓐ most miners became rich

   Ⓑ life did not change for most Californians

   Ⓒ many people moved to California

   Ⓓ no one bought tools

8. John Sutter was building a mill in order to _____.

   Ⓐ cut and sell wood

   Ⓑ make flour

   Ⓒ look for gold

   Ⓓ have a nice place to live

9. Why didn't ships leave from San Francisco?

   Ⓐ The water was frozen.

   Ⓑ No one wanted to leave.

   Ⓒ The tickets for the ships were too expensive.

   Ⓓ No one wanted to work on the ships.

10. After Sutter's workers found gold, Sutter _____.

    Ⓐ thought his mill was a bad idea

    Ⓑ thought his mill was still a good idea

    Ⓒ wanted to move away

    Ⓓ wanted to sell his mill and look for gold

Name_____ Date_____ Score_____

A. VOCABULARY CHECK

Choose a word from the box to complete each sentence.

detests	former	irrigate	satisfied	soil	system

1. Maya put new _____ in the garden so the plants will grow better.

2. A large city needs a good transportation _____ with buses and trains.

3. Farmers have to _____ crops when there is not enough rain.

4. I wasn't very _____ with my test results. I want to try again.

5. Our _____ neighbors came back to visit us.

6. Ron _____ his sister so much that he won't talk to her.

B. COMPREHENSION CHECK

Think about "Harriet Tubman and the Underground Railroad." Fill in the correct bubble.

7. Why did slaves in the South love and respect Harriet Tubman?

    Ⓐ She was a good plantation worker.   Ⓒ She helped hundreds of slaves escape.

    Ⓑ She was a kind slave owner.   Ⓓ She started the Civil War.

8. Tubman went back to the South _____.

    Ⓐ once   Ⓒ 19 times

    Ⓑ three times   Ⓓ only after the Civil War

9. Slave owners in the South _____ Tubman.

    Ⓐ did not know about   Ⓒ hated

    Ⓑ did not care about   Ⓓ laughed about

10. Why did the people in the Underground Railroad help slaves like Tubman?

    Ⓐ They wanted the slaves to work for them.   Ⓒ They were afraid of the slaves.

    Ⓑ They wanted money from the slaves.   Ⓓ They believed that slavery was wrong.

Name_____ Date_____ Score_____

A. VOCABULARY CHECK

Choose a word from the box to complete each sentence.

crevice	enormous	essential	previous	ridge	risky

1. We already learned that information in one of our _____ lessons.

2. Practice is _____ if you want to learn a new language.

3. One of the hikers fell into a(n) _____ and got stuck.

4. Becky's family lives in a(n) _____ house with more than 20 rooms.

5. Driving on the mountain roads at night can be very _____.

6. From the _____ on top of the mountain you can see for miles in every direction.

B. COMPREHENSION CHECK

Think about "A Railroad Unites a Nation." Fill in the correct bubble.

7. Building the railroad to the Pacific was _____.

    (A) easy

    (B) dangerous

    (C) not expensive

    (D) impossible

8. The Union Pacific and Central Pacific built the railroad from Sacramento, California, to _____.

    (A) Promontory Point, Utah

    (B) New York, New York

    (C) Chicago, Illinois

    (D) Omaha, Nebraska

9. Two years after the project started, the Central Pacific _____.

    (A) was almost finished

    (B) stopped working on the railroad

    (C) did not have enough workers

    (D) had too many workers

10. In the end, the manager of the railroad project thought that Chinese workers _____.

    (A) could not do dangerous jobs

    (B) were not hard workers

    (C) were very skillful

    (D) were too small

REPRODUCIBLE

Name_____ Date_____ Score_____

A. VOCABULARY CHECK

Choose a word from the box to complete each sentence.

compromise	conflict	rejected	support	treason	victorious

1. My grandfather _____ the idea of moving into our house. He says he can take care of himself.

2. The _____ team was singing and dancing on the field.

3. You want to meet at 7:00, and I want to meet at 8:00. Let's _____ and meet at 7:30.

4. The spies were found guilty of _____ and sent to prison.

5. I like the governor, but I don't _____ all of his ideas.

6. There is too much _____ in the office. Everyone seems angry and unhappy.

B. COMPREHENSION CHECK

Think about "Surrender at Appomattox." Fill in the correct bubble.

7. When General Lee surrendered to General Grant, Grant _____.

   Ⓐ laughed at Lee
   Ⓑ put Lee in prison
   Ⓒ told his soldiers to shout and cheer
   Ⓓ treated Lee with respect

8. The Union Army from the North _____.

   Ⓐ did not support President Lincoln
   Ⓑ wanted to free the slaves
   Ⓒ wanted to keep slaves
   Ⓓ wanted to leave the United States

9. Grant gave Lee's army _____ because they didn't have any.

   Ⓐ food
   Ⓑ water
   Ⓒ horses and mules
   Ⓓ guns

10. Grant thought Lee was _____.

   Ⓐ a good and honest man
   Ⓑ a very bad man
   Ⓒ a rude man
   Ⓓ a stupid, silly man

Name_____ Date_____ Score_____

A. VOCABULARY CHECK

Choose a word from the box to complete each sentence.

applauded	assassination	declined	image	plot	tragedy

1. *Hamlet* is a famous _____. Nearly everyone is dead at the end.

2. Everyone stood up and _____ at the end of the concert.

3. George Washington's _____ is on the one-dollar bill.

4. After the president's _____, the vice president was made president.

5. I asked Karen if she wanted help, but she _____ my offer.

6. The story is confusing because the _____ is hard to understand.

B. COMPREHENSION CHECK

Think about "Lincoln's Assassination." Fill in the correct bubble.

7. Why did John Wilkes Booth shoot Abraham Lincoln?

  Ⓐ He and Lincoln got in a fight.   Ⓒ He did not like the play.

  Ⓑ He was angry about the Civil War.   Ⓓ He wanted to take Lincoln's money.

8. Why didn't Lincoln's bodyguard protect him at the theater?

  Ⓐ Lincoln's bodyguard refused to go.   Ⓒ Lincoln's bodyguard was part of a conspiracy to kill the president.

  Ⓑ Lincoln didn't have a bodyguard.   Ⓓ Lincoln told his bodyguard not to come.

9. Lincoln died _____.

  Ⓐ in someone else's house   Ⓒ at his home

  Ⓑ in a hospital   Ⓓ in the theater

10. Which sentence about Lincoln is probably true?

  Ⓐ Most Americans were not sad when he was killed.   Ⓒ He was one of the most important U.S. presidents.

  Ⓑ He knew Booth and did not like him.   Ⓓ He did not like going to the theater.

Copyright McGraw-Hill ESL/ELT

Chapter 1

1. inhabitants
2. remote
3. hurricane
4. preserve
5. settle
6. drought
7. C
8. D
9. D
10. A

Chapter 2

1. peninsula
2. cruel
3. rumor
4. permanent
5. ordered
6. canal
7. D
8. B
9. C
10. C

Chapter 3

1. purchased
2. jealous
3. profit
4. customers
5. colonies
6. employer
7. C
8. A
9. D
10. A

Chapter 4

1. wounded
2. tension
3. treaty
4. approval
5. seized
6. hostile
7. C
8. C
9. A
10. A

Chapter 5

1. citizen
2. document
3. candidate
4. representatives
5. debate
6. defeated
7. C
8. B
9. A
10. D

Chapter 6

1. instruments
2. Congress
3. identical
4. capital
5. Supreme Court
6. career
7. B
8. A
9. D
10. B

Chapter 7

1. valley
2. captured
3. courageous
4. desert
5. nutritious
6. journey
7. B
8. C
9. D
10. A

Chapter 8

1. amateur
2. surrender
3. patriotic
4. biography
5. fiction
6. released
7. C
8. A
9. C
10. B

Chapter 9

1. democracy
2. authority
3. survivors
4. loyalty
5. revenge
6. dictatorship
7. B
8. D
9. A
10. C

Chapter 10

1. opposed
2. trial
3. legend
4. accused
5. refused
6. majority
7. D
8. B
9. A
10. D

Chapter 11

1. legislature
2. infection
3. therapy
4. precise
5. eventually
6. radical
7. A
8. B
9. D
10. C

Chapter 12

1. continent
2. doubted
3. Hemisphere
4. influence
5. population
6. departs
7. C
8. A
9. D
10. B

Chapter 13

1. soil
2. system
3. irrigate
4. satisfied
5. former
6. detests
7. C
8. C
9. C
10. D

Chapter 14

1. previous
2. essential
3. crevice
4. enormous
5. risky
6. ridge
7. B
8. D
9. C
10. C

Chapter 15

1. rejected
2. victorious
3. compromise
4. treason
5. support
6. conflict
7. D
8. B
9. A
10. A

Chapter 16

1. tragedy
2. applauded
3. image
4. assassination
5. declined
6. plot
7. B
8. D
9. A
10. C

Get Ready to Read

Answers will vary.

Check Your Understanding

1. Utah, Colorado, Arizona, and New Mexico
2. They climbed ladders.
3. They don't want you to leave trash.

Build Your Vocabulary

1. C
2. A
3. C
4. D
5. B
6. A

Improve Your Reading Skills

1. The Ancient Pueblo people were mysterious. They lived in cliffs.
2. 6
3. Get Ready to Read. It helps students to start thinking about the topic they will read about.
4. 6
5. Check Your Understanding. It helps students see if they have understood the reading.
6. They come from the reading.
7. 4. *Answer will vary according to the student's opinion, but students are likely to consider the words difficult.*
8. Write a paragraph.

Expand Your Vocabulary

1. False
2. False
3. True
4. False

Get Ready to Read

Answers will vary.

Check Your Understanding

1. on the island of Bimini
2. adventurous, cruel, greedy *(other answers possible)*

Build Your Vocabulary

1. A
2. D
3. B
4. C
5. B
6. A

Improve Your Reading Skills

1. made the native people slaves; stole their treasures
2. heard; The native people's stories
3. They quickly followed his directions.
4. ocean; pushing; The ships could not move south easily
5. still there today

Expand Your Vocabulary

1. gulf
2. wetland
3. peninsula
4. canal

Get Ready to Read

Answers will vary.

Check Your Understanding

1. True
2. True
3. False

Build Your Vocabulary

1. A
2. B
3. B
4. D
5. D
6. C

Improve Your Reading Skills

Students will produce artwork.

Expand Your Vocabulary

1. Burger Heaven
2. $10 per hour
3. Ed
4. *The woman in front of the counter should be circled.*

Get Ready to Read

Answers will vary.

Check Your Understanding

1. General Gage brought his troops together.
   →Paul Revere arrived at Lexington.
       →British troops arrived at Concord.
           →British troops returned to Boston.
2. People all over the world learned about what happened in the American colonies.

Build Your Vocabulary

1. B
2. D
3. B
4. C
5. D
6. A

Improve Your Reading Skills

Answers will vary.

Expand Your Vocabulary

1. militia
2. feud
3. hostile
4. treaty

Get Ready to Read

Answers will vary.

Check Your Understanding

1. two weeks
2. to explain the reasons why the colonists wanted to be free from the British
3. People in the United States still are not always treated equally.

Build Your Vocabulary

1. B
2. D
3. C
4. A
5. A
6. D

Improve Your Reading Skills

June 7, 1776: The representatives met in Philadelphia.

July 2, 1776: The representatives voted for independence.

July 4, 1776: The Declaration of Independence was printed.

July 9, 1776: Washington read the Declaration to his army.

1783: The colonists defeated the British.

Expand Your Vocabulary

1. ballot
2. issue
3. candidate
4. citizen

Get Ready to Read

1. **clock maker:** must have knowledge of how clocks work; must be good at making things

   astronomer: must know about stars and planets; must be able to pay close attention to things

   weather forecaster: must know about what causes different kinds of weather; must be able to use information to guess about future weather

   city designer / planner: must know about everything that is needed in a city; must have artistic ability and organizational skills

2. *Answers will vary.*

Check Your Understanding

1. a watch
2. his almanacs
3. He taught himself to make clocks and made the first striking clock in America.

   He taught himself math and astronomy and wrote almanacs.

   He taught himself map-making and helped design Washington, D.C.

Build Your Vocabulary

1. D
2. B
3. C
4. D
5. A
6. B

Improve Your Reading Skills

1. Banneker's life was changed.
2. He borrowed instruments from a friend and cut a hole in his roof.
3. He became famous in the United States, England, and France.
4. L'Enfant (the designer) was fired.
5. Banneker remembered the plans and drew them again.

Expand Your Vocabulary

1. Supreme Court
2. Congress
3. House of Representatives
4. Senate

Get Ready to Read

Answers will vary.

Check Your Understanding

1. They had a girl and her baby with them.
2. horses, supplies, and guides
3. It was too difficult and cold to travel during the winter.

Build Your Vocabulary

1. C
2. D
3. B
4. A
5. C
6. C

Improve Your Reading Skills

The explorers left St. Louis in May 1804. Several months later, Sacagawea joined the group. Later on, Sacagawea saved valuable papers and supplies when a boat sank. Then the Shoshone chief gave the explorers what they needed to cross the mountains. Finally, Lewis and Clark reached the Pacific Ocean.

Expand Your Vocabulary

1. prairie
2. valley
3. canyon
4. desert

Get Ready to Read

Answers will vary.

Check Your Understanding

1. **Who:** Francis Scott Key
    When: September 14, 1814
    Where: on a ship in Baltimore Harbor, Maryland
    Why: to show Key's excitement and love for his country

2. It was important to see the flag because the flag showed that the Americans were still in the fort. It meant that the United States was not defeated.

Build Your Vocabulary

1. C
2. B
3. C
4. B
5. C
6. A

Improve Your Reading Skills

Answers will vary.

Expand Your Vocabulary

1. nonfiction
2. biography
3. fiction
4. autobiography

Get Ready to Read

Answers will vary.

Check Your Understanding

1. General Antonio López de Santa Anna
2. They fired a cannon ball and began to fight.
3. They were angry about what happened at the Alamo and wanted to punish the Mexican army for it.

Build Your Vocabulary

1. C
2. B
3. D
4. D
5. A
6. B

Improve Your Reading Skills

1. about 1820
2. a. The Americans were used to governing themselves.
   b. The Americans did not speak Spanish.
   c. The Americans did not belong to the Catholic Church.
3. Santa Anna told the captain to surrender.
4. 12 days

Expand Your Vocabulary

1. anarchy
2. monarchy
3. democracy
4. dictatorship

Get Ready to Read

Answers will vary.

Check Your Understanding

1. They refused to leave and took their case to the U.S. Supreme Court.
2. the fall and winter
3. The people in Georgia now realize that what they did to the Cherokees was wrong, and they wanted to honor the Cherokees.

Build Your Vocabulary

1. C
2. A
3. D
4. A
5. D
6. A

Improve Your Reading Skills

1. D
2. A

Expand Your Vocabulary

1. False
2. False
3. True
4. False

Get Ready to Read

Answers will vary.

Check Your Understanding

1. Massachusetts
2. proper care
3. She did not want to become famous and did her work because she really cared about mentally ill people.

Build Your Vocabulary

1. D
2. A
3. A
4. D
5. B
6. B

Improve Your Reading Skills

1. **Main Idea:** The conditions in the jail were awful.

   Supporting Detail: There was no heat or fresh air.

   Supporting Detail: Cells were dirty and smelled terrible.

   Supporting Detail: Prisoners were treated cruelly. Some were beaten.

2. **Main Idea:** Dix began collecting facts to show to people in the Massachusetts government.

   Supporting Detail: In one town, a mentally ill woman was kept in a small cage.

   Supporting Detail: In another town, one mentally ill prisoner was chained, while another was kept in a small room for 17 years.

   Supporting Detail: In a third town, two mentally ill women lay on straw in wooden beds.

Expand Your Vocabulary

1. vaccinate
2. fever
3. infection
4. therapy

Get Ready to Read

Answers will vary.

Check Your Understanding

1. He was going to cut down trees to make and sell lumber.
2. He wanted to finish building his mill without people looking for gold nearby.
3. There were not enough shovels, so they were very valuable. People thought that they could use a shovel to find gold worth more than $20.

Build Your Vocabulary

1. C
2. B
3. C
4. A
5. C
6. A

Improve Your Reading Skills

1. d
2. a
3. c
4. e
5. b

Expand Your Vocabulary

1. pole *or* North Pole
2. continent
3. equator
4. hemisphere *or* Southern Hemisphere

Get Ready to Read

Answers will vary.

Check Your Understanding

1. She wanted to make herself look like a man so slave owners would not recognize her. It was probably less unusual for a man to be traveling alone than a woman.
2. No one was likely to look for an escaped slave going south. They probably expected her to go north.
3. She was a spy for the Union army.

Build Your Vocabulary

1. B   4. D
2. C   5. B
3. A   6. A

Improve Your Reading Skills

Vocabulary	Context Clues	What do the clues tell about the meaning of the vocabulary word?
routes	— Underground Railroad … name for secret routes for slave to escape to the North	— like a railroad, but not a railroad — Slaves used routes to escape.
satisfied	— not satisfied just to be free herself; she wanted to do more	— When you are not satisfied, you want to change things.
system	— system of barns, caves, and homes …	— The system had many parts.
former	— of her former owner, where she used to be a slave	— "former" describes something that used to be true.
detested	— Slave owners detested Tubman and offered $40,000 for her capture. However, the slaves respected her …	— People who detested Tubman wanted to capture her. — "However" shows that "detest" is very different from "respect."
abolished	— abolish slavery, making all people in the United States free	— Abolishing slavery made it end or go away.

Expand Your Vocabulary

1. True   3. False
2. False   4. True

Get Ready to Read

Answers will vary.

Check Your Understanding

1. government money and land
2. the Union Pacific and the Central Pacific
3. The managers did not believe they could do a good job.

Build Your Vocabulary

1. A
2. D
3. B
4. D
5. A
6. C

Improve Your Reading Skills

1. Fact
2. Opinion
3. Opinion
4. Fact
5. Fact
6. Opinion
7. Fact
8. Opinion

Expand Your Vocabulary

1. plateau
2. crevice
3. ridge
4. plain

Get Ready to Read

Answers will vary.

Check Your Understanding

1. They needed the animals to plant spring crops.
2. He asked for food for his men.
3. He thought cheering did not show respect for the Southern army, and he wanted all Americans to get along again.

Build Your Vocabulary

1. D
2. A
3. C
4. C
5. B
6. D

Improve Your Reading Skills

1. Lee ordered his army out of the city.
2. Grant knew it was dangerous to allow Lee's army to rest and get new supplies.
3. Lee decided to surrender.
4. President Lincoln ordered Grant not to punish anyone in the defeated army.

Expand Your Vocabulary

1. conflict
2. diplomatic
3. negotiate
4. compromise

Get Ready to Read

Answers will vary.

Check Your Understanding

1. He wanted to forget about the war and other bad things. He wanted to make his wife happy.
2. He said that the bodyguard had worked a long, hard day and should go home.
3. nine hours

Build Your Vocabulary

1. D
2. A
3. D
4. C
5. A
6. B

Improve Your Reading Skills

1. B
2. D
3. C
4. C
5. A

Expand Your Vocabulary

1. script
2. plot
3. villain
4. tragedy

Workshop I (Pages 13-14)

1. B
2. B
3. B
4. C
5. *Answers will vary according to the dictionary used.*
6. noun
7–9. *Answers will vary according to the dictionary used.*

Workshop II (Pages 27-28)

S. D
1. B
2. D
3. C
4. A

Workshop III (Pages 41-42)

1. not fair
2. understood wrong
3. view again
4. view before
5. not dependent
6. unkind, not kind
7. rebuild, build again
8. misread, read wrong
   reread, read again
9. incomplete, not complete
10. full of beauty
11. able to be enjoyed
12. someone who governs
13. without life
14. process of explaining
15. connection, result of being connected
16. teachable, able to be taught
    teacher, someone who teaches
17. cheerful, full of cheer
    cheerless, without cheer
18. thoughtful, full of thought
    thoughtless, without thought

Workshop IV (Pages 55-56)

S1. A
S2. D
S3. C
S4. C

1. D
2. D
3. C
4. B

5. A
6. B
7. C
8. A

Workshop V (Pages 69-70)

1. c
2. i
3. g
4. b
5. h
6. e
7. j
8. d
9. a (Although most dictionaries give different pronunciations for *pedal* and *petal*, in American English they are indeed homophones.)
10. f

1. here
2. one
3. petals
4. weak
5. scent
6. break
7. there
8. peace
9. hall
10. wait
11. cents
12. their
13. pedal
14. piece
15. won
16. hear
17. brakes
18. weight
19. haul
20. week

Workshop VI (Pages 83-84)

S1. C
S2. B

1. A
2. D
3. A
4. A
5. C
6. D

Workshop VII (Pages 97-98)

1. (2) the situation of being with someone
2. (3) a business
3. (1) a guest or guests at your home
4. (4) a unit of soldiers
5. *Answers will vary.*
6. *Answers will vary.*

1. 2
2. 1
3. 5
4. 3
5. 4
6. 2
7–10. *Answers will vary according to the dictionary used.*

Workshop VIII (Pages 111-112)

S1. C
S2. A
S3. A
S4. D

1. B
2. C
3. A
4. D
5. D
6. A